I0530231

"John Dorsey's book is a tribute to small town life. He carefully dissects the lives of his characters to find the crossroads where dreams were thwarted, and how the survivors of these lost dreams manage to carry on anyway, sometimes as though they don't even know how close they came to escaping the bear trap of smoky bars and bar fights and the endless cycle of pregnancy and childrearing. Each inhabitant of these poems is treated with delicate dignity, leaving you with the feeling that you've met each and every one of these characters at some point in your own life, or may have even been in one of two of these poems yourself."

-Holly Day, author of *Into the Cracks*

"John Dorsey is one of my favorite living poets - clear minute particulars and broken-hearted honesty. Generous empathetic outlook for our hardened times."

-Marc Olmsted, author of *Don't Hesitate: Knowing Allen Ginsberg*

Dead Photographs

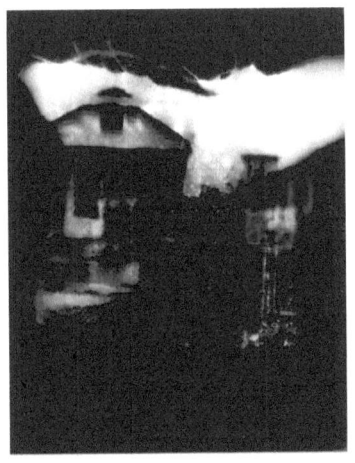

Poems by John Dorsey

Stubborn Mule Press

Devil's Elbow, Missouri

Copyright © John Dorsey, 2024
First Edition: 1 3 5 7 9 10 8 6 4 2
ISBN: 978-1-958182-85-7
LCCN: 2024944487
Cover image: Louis-Jacques-Mandé Daguerre
Title page image: Unknown
Author photo: John Dorsey

Acknowledgments

These pieces are works of erasure crafted from the poems of Barry Gifford, full credit is given where credit is due. Thanks is also given to the board & staff of Osage Arts Community, where these pieces were created.

Table of Contents

For Mike James, who showed me
this was possible.

Dead Photographs

Pure

the sky in 1958
is a ghost.

Winter

our bodies fail
in the snow.

This Morning

the past
is a rare
white cocoon.

Sore Throat

the rain softly
took your voice.

Friday Night

> still alive
> a storm
> whiteknuckled time
> pillows didn't matter.

The Riverside

touched my cock
with some difficulty.

The Train

flickering in
the warm lonely dark.

Beautiful Cold Sunlight

wouldn't leave
a young girl
never young again.

Imagining Women

in the light rain.

Furious Summer Sun

total loss.

Sleeping City

astonished mountains
waving.

No Know

dangle
the ground.

So Many Bridges

are beautiful.

A River

flowers
nobody notices.

Frozen Nose

sky
staring
at winter.

Mad Birds

diving along
ragged.

You

often alone
without a face
a young girl
missing.

Your White Body

a frightened horse.

Small Town

late night leafs
fluttering lonely shape
radiant shadow
under a blue beret.

Hotel Window

baudelaire
listening
to cars honking.

Darling

you died alone
on the moon's
birthday.

Your Beautiful Asshole

raised on
the stove.

I Always Loved

your shadow
the picture
of your family.

Perfect Form

her open mouth
amazes me.

Two Lovers

reminded
of muddy denim jackets.

A Woman Walking

with a big rear end
constantly disappointed.

Rain

around your waist
trees suddenly reminded.

Snowflakes Curled

your mind cold
dawn settling
under the bed.

The Rain

fingering herself
above an open window.

An Old Girlfriend

a giant alligator
leaving her clothes again.

Nobody

devoured his dreams
crocodiles forgot constantly.

Children Giving Birth

the sun threatens
the restless winter.

Hobos & Shamans

the only prayers
created
of hatred.

A Deer Gone

his head eaten
lucky for him.

The Mountain Fog

a rabbit
a bird
a night
before men.

A Woman

on a corner
never exists.

A Beautiful Girl

my hand
on her leg.

The Door

stuck out
like your cunt
40 years ago.

Stardust

i still remember rory calhoun
a piano blocking
the backyard.

I Don't Remember Love

everything
waiting.

The Wind

sucked out
like a woodpecker
twisting.

Morning Sun

the sun
pays no attention
to november.

A Coyote

not a large dog
recognized in us
that sense of ecstasy.

Jack Spicer is a Good Game

anybody interested
in their rivals
are the ghosts
of disturbing purpose.

Dream Boy

moon
namesake
i summon you
old man.

Jack Spicer was a Speeding Train

if babe ruth was still alive
think about the off-season.

Men Devour

the tender waitress
her body splinters
over the horizon.

Woman Waiting

for the bus
all night
dance & sway
in the rain.

Horses Sipping Tea

are vulnerable
birds tilt
on the hillside.

She was Crazy

& lost it
in bed.

Bodies

      in the october sun
      buried under red trees.

In a Rainy Gutter

paranoid last words
say nothing
you never find your destiny
at the body-less piano.

Each Day

old eyes
serious red sun.

Rain Coming Down

so warm
without saying
i wanted you.

Dead White Pigeons

my cat on her belly
looking around
at evening
such an
unbelievable beauty.

Not Enough Sunlight

good days are short
poems are written
in the afternoon rain
lying in bed.

Protect Sweat & Shit

immunity is temporary.

A Curious Note

blood-red swans are rare
the sun beats with disgust.

Eyes Gleaming

anything is possible for an instant
you will forget
the loveliest hour.

A Whore Died a Virgin

we never made love
we remember sad history.

No Birds

a handful of sun
bones leave you
on the mountain.

Lunch

in 1959
a sidewalk
a small boy
passed out
down the street
the smell of papaya.

Kissed Off Yesterday

a dishonest girlfriend died
in a photo
i remembered
she had
a beautiful laugh.

In a Hotel Room

he missed his lovely daughter
by taking
his own life.

A Faded Beauty

i imagine pretty girls
bums reading their eyes
feigning disinterest
like a powerful telescope of squeals
a museum no longer dead.

The Wild Girl

naked with
imagination
only sees the point
of madness.

A Beautiful Girl

the earth spinning
makes perfect sense.

His Old Man

skinny dog circling
under the tree.

This Perfect Room

of whispering blondes
in a ghost dream.

Few Faces

disappear as easily
as rain.

Sparrows in Our Backyard

as precise
as leaning
haystacks.

No Weather

or birds
lovers slowly settle.

Simple

you escape
the sound
of your voice.

Afternoon Pillow

the sun is
never enough.

Rose Died

so nice of her
to visit me
wearing a white nightgown.

The Sky

in a black & white movie
with you

such colors.

Older Women

remind me
of a straw hat
my mother used to wear
on the beach.

Florida Keys

you haunted my dreams
in a red dress.

Sitting Naked

i wonder through so many years
an open window
of difficult things.

Through This Rain

another woman
reassuring
like the light.

One Strange Eye

a stone
in the shape of a heart
looks new.

Wasting Time

the dog sings
a kind of bird
barking thoughts
just before light.

A Suitcase & a Bag

a girl carrying
her right eye
back to ohio
died fifty-three years ago
in a photograph.

You've Been in Love

on a busy street
a return address
people don't forget.

I Used to Live with Jazz

goldfinches in the trees
on a rainy day
a better poem
is enough.

When Hedy Lamarr was No Longer Young

the burden of being a great beauty
was an impossible photograph
on the wall.

The Last Big House

was finally dark
there was no moon
no fireflies slowly flickering
from thought to thought
moment to moment.

Coltrane, 1957

six months of beauty
just died.

Dead People

take your suitcase
neither young
nor old

it starts to rain fire
your family gone
outside.

Women & Death

dangerous memories
are gone.

Your Mother's Funeral in the Bar

a glass filled with a dry martini
in the ugliest town
a woman's expression
unchanged.

Dead Photographs

you didn't let me touch you
your clothes were made
out of dead photographs.

Seventeen Years Ago

her name was beautiful
in later years
she ordered a martini in japan
at least twenty
or thirty.

One Strange Eye #2

i approach roses
in fresh water
with one strange eye
at the foot
of a heart.

On the Day of Your Death

you thirst for beauty
that last bit of sun.

The Happiest Man

could not
shed the sentiment
to fool a sparrow
in the darkening afternoon.

Heart like the Sun

a bird singing in your dream
would have been impolite
long ago
things were different.

I Saw a Girl with Lost Fingers

she was very pretty
she's been dead for years
we shook hands
said thanks
neither of us
was in love.

A Gloomy Woman

smiling perfectly
burst into flames
on the corner
for the first time
in months.

Role Reversal

a rose
the size
of a bee.

Her Lovers

her loose right eye
sitting on a stool
her lovers took her body
dreaming of red apples.

In 1939

edward hopper
sent me everything

bette davis
painting over
true love.

A Rather Sad History

it's likely baudelaire
never made love
to love poems

& died
a virgin.

Modern Work

is a box of coal
grey chestnut trees
draped in the courtyard.

The Other Women

wish to disappear
laughing white teeth
having died
become invisible
a shy mountain
of long black hair.

In the City

the world
hates wet streets
a murky country road
nobody changes
the movies.

Love Didn't Die

his last words
were fired back
into the harbor.

Beauty Made Sense From Death

no past
no future.

James Dean's Red Ribbon

is the movie
of suffering.

Long Fingers of Riverline

it's america

a girl
a car
no sound
in the rain.

Frank Johnson Never
Made Me Cry

his wife died young
she was wild & kind
never beautiful
mostly gone
i can still picture her.

Lingering Rainy Morning

two days
before my dreams appear
i recognize
her white ghost.

Bored People

will be there
these women are lizards.

In Front of the River

a postcard of moving parts
bruised faces
in the painting.

He Time Traveled
to South America

his camera
published his own demise
no longer
in search
of souls.

Seeing the Photographs

i wrote you a little today
old times
remember
it's dangerous
to make sense.

His Dead Wife

with a monkey
on her shoulder
answers quickly.

Dead Men

their minds
have plenty of room
to be foolish.

Robert Duncan was Gone

back to his house
in the harbor
the canon
running
down the street.

Mary Lou at the Oakland Airport

i was a kid
from the old perry mason tv show
just off a plane.

My Shoulders in Front of an Open Coffin

her eyes reminded me of death
her nose turned away.

We Were Both There

paul & i hated hippies
& mountains
we swam
looking for
an old hotel.

Death

murdered his lawyer
with certainty.

One Country Called Americana

his long beard
a few pennies
a snowy street
a lost story
in his journal.

These Freaks He Created

his bizarre sad poems
spoke only silence.

A Conversation

he believed in me
that's small potatoes
he smiled
reaching for my thoughts
in the air.

Her Shoulders

her knees
her way of life
idealized nothing
more beautiful.

Marylou & I

there for the holiday
your father wearing a brown suit
in 1957.

Regardless of the Ocean

steady wind
slow waves
she was pretty too.

The Most Beautiful Friends

dirty hair
porcelain skin
stunned
i fled
the sidewalk.

I Have a Photograph

of chicago
where rose once played the piano
& sang
in front
of a palm tree.

There is Seldom a Point

just memories
that end
badly.

Swimming in Dark Stars

dexter gordon threading water
somewhere in europe
calling from the shore.

The Last Good Weather

a notebook
a blue peacoat
a sparrow.

You Don't Need to Listen

to river music
the rest
of the afternoon
demands
your attention.

In Those Days

in sweaters
coats
& caps
kids drove away
alone
older.

All Weekend

you embraced me
a drugstore kiss
another surprise
no one knows enough.

I'll Go Back to Paris

the river almost crazy
an old friend.

Up Before the Sun

most days
thinking about
proust's boys
beautiful faces in 1954
coffee
fruit
toast
i've done
none of it.

Cervantes' Highest Branch

he's not
still alive
crouched below
asleep on a knife.

Robert Taylor Shot a Paper Gun

a wild woman
must have something to lose
some words ambushed
in this morning's paper.

Without Too Much Piano

some of us are a ghost
nothing in plain sight
summer is lipstick
& chop suey
elegies exist in my head
poems don't end.

John Dorsey is the former Poet Laureate of Belle, MO. He is the author of several collections of poetry, including *Which Way to the River: Selected Poems: 2016-2020* (OAC Books, 2020), *Sundown at the Redneck Carnival,* (Spartan Press, 2022, and *Pocatello Wildflower,* (Crisis Chronicles Press, 2023). He may be reached at archerevans@ yahoo.com.

www.ingramcontent.com/pod-product-compliance
Lightning Source LLC
Chambersburg PA
CBHW031529120626
46545CB00005B/2067